FAVOR
God's Exception to the Rule

By

Rolanda Gibson & Shenetha Caldwell

Copyright 2020 © Rolanda Gibson. All Rights Reserved.

This book may not be reproduced in whole or part, in any form or by any means, electronic or mechanical, including photocopying, recording, or by any information storage and retrieval system now known hereafter invented, without the written permission of the publisher.

Unless otherwise indicated, all scripture quotations are taken from the King James Version of the Bible.

Published by Rolanda Gibson Ministries

ISBN: 978-0-578-64307-6

Acknowledgements

To the Holy Spirit who is my teacher, guide, and comforter. Thank you for faithfully leading me into all truth.

To my parents Thomas and Rose Gibson. Words cannot express how blessed I am to have you as my parents. Thank you for believing in me, supporting me, and loving me unconditionally. I will always love you!

To my pastors Drs. Guevara and Shannon Johnson. Thank you for unapologetically teaching the Word of God with integrity, boldness, and without compromise. I love and appreciate you both.

~Rolanda

Acknowledgements

First, I thank God that He is Lord over my life. So grateful that He has favored and chosen me. He is the Source of my life. Thank You Lord for giving me grace beyond measure, favor, strength, and most of all for giving me life more abundantly. To my mother who is always there, thank you. I love you dearly. To my children who have always been an inspiration to me, you keep me going. Thanks young men, I love you all dearly.

Thank you Bishop Danny and Dr. Carolyn Hunt for praying, covering, correcting, mentoring, and nurturing me. The example you set as leaders is unexplainable. I love you dearly.

~Shenetha

FAVOR: God's Exception to the Rule

Table of Contents

Acknowledgements..4 & 5

Opening Prayer...7

Introduction...8

Understanding God's Favor......................................11

The Purpose of Favor..17

Paying the Price..23

FAVOR: God's Exception to the Rule..........................31

Access Granted: The Influence of Favor......................35

Principles of Favor...39

The Finishing Touch...47

About the Authors..63-65

Opening Prayer

Father in the name of Jesus, I thank You for this opportunity to strengthen the wisdom, knowledge and favor You have given me. I pray that upon reading this book, favor will become common in my life. Father, Your Word says in *II Chronicles 16:9a "for the eyes of the Lord run to and fro throughout the whole earth, to shew Himself strong in the behalf of them whose heart is perfect toward Him."* Lord I am fully committed to You and my heart is fully surrendered to You. I ask that You pour out your favor upon me this day and manifest it in every area of my life. In Jesus name, amen!

FAVOR: God's Exception to the Rule

Introduction

"But there is a spirit in man: and the inspiration of the Almighty giveth them understanding." (Job 32:8)

"I'm blessed and highly favored!" "Favor ain't fair!" "I'm walking in God's favor!" "God is shifting things in my favor!" If I've heard them once, I've heard them a thousand times, familiar clichés quoted by well meaning Christians as a way of declaring that God's favor is operating in their lives. But when I hear these responses along with others, I often wonder if the people who've said them really understand what it means to have the favor. Do they understand the purpose of favor? The responsibility of favor? The cost of favor?

The favor of God has always been, and still is a "hot topic" in the body of Christ. It is one of the most talked about yet misunderstood topics in the church today. Many times when people think of God's favor, they think of it in the natural or materialistic sense. Associating it more with possessions and wealth rather than purpose and destiny. Now don't misunderstand me, in some instances, having material possessions is a direct result of having God's favor, but we must

Introduction

understand that the favor of God is not given so we can buy houses, land, automobiles and acquire other worldly possessions and then declare "favor ain't fair" and "I'm blessed and highly favored." No, God's favor is given as a strategic tool to carry out His specific purpose and plan for our lives.

Having God's favor is one thing, understanding His purpose and plan for giving us favor is another. *FAVOR: God's Exception to the Rule,* is designed to introduce, explain and reveal the favor of God in such a way that you have a clear understanding of the meaning, purpose, and plan of God's favor. This book is also designed to help you walk in your God given favor while learning to deal with the consequences (jealousy, envy, rejection, isolation, etc.) and the responsibilities that come as a result of being favored by God.

Everything God does, He does out of purpose. When He gives us His favor, it's not so we can gain popularity, riches or power, but so that the lives of others can be changed, and so that He can be glorified. I pray that as you read this book, God will enlighten the eyes of your understanding as it relates to His favor, speak to you about His purpose for giving you favor, and teach you how to use His favor to fulfill your purpose.

FAVOR: God's Exception to the Rule

Father in the name of Jesus, I thank You now for the ability to understand what Your favor is and what it is not. You said in Deuteronomy 11:26-27 "Behold, I set before you this day a blessing and a curse; A blessing, if ye obey the commandments of the Lord your God, which I command you this day:" Lord, As I obey and follow Your Word, teach me how to walk in Your favor, and bless me with increased favor with God and man. In Jesus name, Amen.

Chapter 1

Understanding the Favor of God

"But there is a spirit in a man: and the inspiration of the Almighty giveth them understanding. (Job 32:8)

One of the greatest assets a Believer can have is the favor of God. It is a God given gift that is more valuable than silver, gold, diamonds, rubies or any other precious stone you can name. It cannot be bought, sold, or earned; but it is freely given by God to His children according to His good pleasure, and according to His purpose and plan for our lives.

Having God's favor is a tremendous blessing that should never be taken for granted; and those who have it should desire to experience all of the benefits and privileges that are available as a result of having God's favor. But in order to do that, we must clearly understand what the favor of God is AND what it is not. The best way to do this is by understanding the word favor.

FAVOR: God's Exception to the Rule

By gaining insight of the word favor, we can develop a better understanding of the favor of God. There are many definitions for the word favor, but I'll share with you the three that I believe are the most significant.

Definition 1

Favor is the underserved kindness of God given solely because of His generosity. Approval. Unfair partiality. Preferential treatment. To endorse.

Definition 2

Favor is the special affection of God towards someone that releases an influence on them so that others are inclined to like and/or cooperate with them.

Definition 3

Favor is the guarantee of God's presence, and the provision of His power to accomplish His special purpose in and through our lives.

By using the definitions that were just given, we can conclude that the favor of God is: (1) given solely because of His generosity and His good pleasure; (2) gives us influence with others so that we can fulfill our God given assignments and (3)

Understanding the Favor of God

guarantees us God's presence and power as we work to accomplish His purpose and plan in and through our lives.

Understanding the favor of God is very important; however, understanding what God's favor is NOT is just as important. Contrary to popular opinion, and contrary to some erroneous biblical teachings, the favor of God is not a spiritual version of a genie in a bottle. Some of you may disagree with the scenarios I'm about to present, but it is important to shed light on them so we can put God's favor back into proper perspective. There are many examples I can use, but I'll use the following three to help me address what the favor of God is NOT.

Example 1

Finding a parking spot in the front of a store on a busy shopping day is not the favor OF God. I cannot tell you how many times I've heard people make this statement and ones similar to it and attribute it to having God's favor.

Example 2

Being moved from the back of a long line to the front of the line at a local restaurant is not the favor OF God. The manager, who is your friend, family member or church member noticed you at the back of the line and brought you to the front. I hate to disappoint you, but this is not an indication that the favor OF God is on your life.

Example 3

When a salesperson applies their employee discount to your purchase without you asking them to is not the favor OF God operating in your life.

Acknowledging God and giving Him the glory for the good things He gives us, and for the good things He allows to take place in our life should be done with joy and without hesitation, that is our reasonable service; but saying those things happened because we have the favor OF God can be misleading and cause confusion as to what the favor OF God really is. I believe that many times, what we say is the favor OF God is actually a favor FROM God. Allow me to say that again. Many times, what we say is the favor OF God is actually a favor FROM God. The favor OF God is not the same as a favor FROM God.

Consider for a moment the difference between the two. The favor OF God is given so we can accomplish His purpose and plan for our lives. It's a tool given to help us gain access to the necessary people, places and things so we can complete our God given assignments. Although we do benefit from having the favor OF God, it's not given for our convenience or comfort. A favor FROM God is given or done for our convenience, comfort or enjoyment, and it is not necessarily connected to God's assignment for our life. The favor of God is not hard to understand, but it is often misunderstood and taken out of perspective because many times what people want isn't the favor OF God for His purpose, but rather favors FROM God for their convenience.

The favor of God is a valuable asset in the life of a Believer, and in order to maximize it and experience all of the benefits associated with it, you must have a clear and accurate understanding as to what it is and what it is not. Having God's favor is one thing, but understanding God's favor is everything.

FAVOR: God's Exception to the Rule

Father I thank You now that as I follow You, You will lead me into a place of fulfillment in my life. You said in John 16:13a "howbeit when He, the Spirit of truth, is come, He will guide you into all truth." Lord, I ask that you teach me how to operate in the favor You have given me and use it as a tool to help me fulfill Your purpose for my life. In Jesus name, Amen.

Chapter 2

The Purpose of Favor

"Then Mordecai commanded to answer Esther, think not with thyself that thou shalt escape in the king's house, more than all the Jews. For if thou altogether holdest thy peace at this time, then shall enlargement and deliverance arise to the Jews from another place; but thou and thy father's house shall be destroyed: and who knoweth whether thou are come to the kingdom for such a time as this?" (Esther 4:13-14)

"The greatest tragedy in life is not death, but life without a purpose. It is dangerous to be alive and not know why you were given life "~Myles Munroe. Why are you here? What is your purpose? What is the assignment God has created you for? Anointed you for? Favored you for? It may not seem like it, but your answer to these questions can give you a glimpse into the reason God's favor is on your life: or the reason He desires to put His favor on your life.

FAVOR: God's Exception to the Rule

Knowing your purpose in life is essential to understanding the purpose of having God's favor. The favor of God on your life as a Believer is directly connected to God's purpose or assignment for your life. Although we do enjoy the benefits of having God's favor, His favor is not given for our enjoyment, neither is it given to accomplish our own agenda. The favor of God is given for the sole purpose of accomplishing His agenda and carrying out His ordained assignment for our life.

In this chapter, we will examine the life of Queen Esther to help us gain greater insight as to how having God's favor helps us accomplish His purpose for our lives. The Bible says in *Romans 2:11 "for there is no respect of persons with God."* When it comes to working through people to fulfill His purpose in the earth, God does not play favorites. Everyone has a job to do. However, as we'll soon discover, there are some assignments that are so significant to God, that He clearly singles out some people over others to get the job done. Esther was one of those people!

With a destiny that would take her from orphan to queen, the favor of God wasted no time positioning and preparing Esther to fulfill God's purpose for her life. Now, I stated in the introduction that the favor of God is a strategic tool that is designed to help us complete God's assignment for our lives.

The Purpose of Favor

However, we must realize that before favor helps us fulfill purpose, it must first take us through a process. When Esther arrived at the palace, she didn't immediately walk into her purpose; but, God's favor started working immediately to get her ready for her purpose. I believe the life of Esther reveals to us a three step process that God's favor takes us through to move us closer to fulfilling our purpose. Let's use the scriptures to identify and discuss this three step process.

The Bible says in *Esther 2:9a (NLT), "Hegai was very impressed with Esther and treated her kindly. He quickly ordered a special menu for her and provide her with beauty treatments."* The first step in the process of favor is **provision.** Favor provides us with the tools we need to move us towards accomplishing our God given assignment. To prepare for her night with the king, Esther needed a special menu, maid, and items for purification. Not only did favor provide her with what she needed, but it was quickly provided. Vs. 9 says that *"Esther gained favor with Hegai (the keeper of the women).* As a result, he quickly provided her with the things she needed.

Favor operates in our life the same way. Whether it's a college education, a business loan, a higher paying job or favor with your supervisor; God will use the favor that is on our life to provide us with everything we need to move us closer to fulfilling His purpose for our life.

The second step in the process of favor is also found in vs. 9. Let's look at the second part of that verse. Vs. 9b says *"and he preferred her and her maids unto the best place of the house of the women."* The second step is **position.** As He did with Esther, God will allow the favor He has on our life to position us in the best location or situation to give us every advantage to fulfill our purpose. Sometimes, being in the right position may mean having to relocate to a new city or state. It may mean having to leave one church to join another. It can also mean no longer associating with certain family members or friends because of their influence to pull us back into a lifestyle God has already delivered us from. Position is an important element in completing our assignment. We cannot fulfill our purpose if we are in the wrong position.

The third and final step in the process of favor is **promotion.** *Esther 2:17* says *"and the king loved Esther above all the women, and she obtained grace and favor in his sight more than all the virgins; so that he set the royal crown upon her head, and made her queen instead of Vashti."*

The Purpose of Favor

Although they are different, steps two and three are interconnected. Step two deals with position, while step three deals with promotion; however, we must realize that promotion involves position. Let me explain. God will position us (step 2), to promote us to the position (step 3) that's attached to our purpose.

For example, God may allow you to get laid off from your job at Company A, so you can be hired at Company B (step 2 position) where He has a specific purpose for you. After working a few months at Company B, you are promoted (step 3 promotion) to the position of Supervisor which is the position God needed you in to fulfill His purpose for sending you to Company B. So God has to position us, to promote us to the position that's connected to our purpose.

Esther being promoted to the position of Queen was the final step in the process of favor. Her purpose was to save the Jews from annihilation, and God's favor allowed her to be promoted to the position of queen in order to accomplish His purpose for her life. The favor of God in the life of a Believer has a specific and undeniable purpose. It is not for our benefit and enjoyment, but for the completion of God's agenda for our life. Favor without purpose is like faith without works, dead!

FAVOR: God's Exception to the Rule

Our Father in heaven, I am grateful that you are a God who will never leave me nor forsake me. You said in your Word "but the God of all grace, who hath called us unto His eternal glory by Christ Jesus, after that ye have suffered a while, make you perfect, stablish, strengthen, settle you" (I Peter 5:10). Lord I thank you for the strength to endure the process and hardships that come as a result of having your favor. I know that when I suffer for your name's sake, there is an eternal glory that awaits me. Lord, as I pay the price for having your favor, help me to represent you well. In Jesus name, Amen!

Chapter 3

Paying the Price

"You will find that everything in life has a price, and you will have to decide whether the price is worth the prize" ~Unknown

Are you willing to pay the price for having God's favor? Are you willing to deal with the consequences that are associated with having the favor of God? Oftentimes, we excitedly declare that favor isn't fair, while failing to realize that favor isn't free! Many people want the prize (God's favor), but only a few are willing and able to pay the price. Anything of value that is worth having will cost us a price, and the favor of God is no different.

In the natural realm, the price of something is calculated and determined using dollars and cents; but in the spiritual realm, the price of something is calculated and determined by God's purpose for our life, the sacrifices we're willing to make, and the persecution we face. The greater God's purpose is for your life,

FAVOR: God's Exception to the Rule

the greater the sacrifices you will have to make, and the greater the persecution you will experience.

From Genesis to Revelation, we can find numerous examples of men and women of God who paid the price for having God's favor. Joseph was despised by his brothers. So much so that they stripped him of his special coat, sold him into slavery and allowed their father to believe he was dead. David was belittled by his brothers and overlooked by his father when Samuel came to anoint the new king. He was also despised by king Saul who tried to take his life because he was jealous of David's anointing and favor.

Daniel was hated by the presidents and princes of king Darius because of the wisdom and favor of God that was on his life. They hated him so much until they tricked the king into passing a decree that specifically targeted Daniel's relationship with God, and when he refused to comply with the decree, he was cast into the den of lions. But that wasn't the end of the story, because the same favor that caused Daniel to be cast into the den of lions, was the same favor that delivered him from the den of lions. Favor is always costly. No, it may not cause us to be sold into slavery, it may not require us to go in hiding because someone is trying to take our life, and it may not cause us to be thrown into a den of lions, but it will cost us something.

Paying the Price

There's a quote that says *"the hardest walk is walking alone but it's also the walk that makes you the strongest."* Rejection is another way people pay the price for having God's favor. This spirit of rejection often causes the recipients of God's favor to walk a lonely road; but though the road is lonely, we are never along. Jesus said in *Matthew 28:20b "and, lo, I am with you always, even unto the end of the world."*

Maybe you've been belittled and overlooked like David, or hated by your siblings like Joseph. Perhaps, like Daniel, people have tried to set destructive traps for you because they were jealous and envious of the favor of God that is on your life; or maybe you've experienced rejection from family, friends or co-workers. At any rate, paying the price for favor comes in many forms; but as we learn from the lives of Joseph (who was promoted to Prime Minister in Egypt), David (who was anointed and became King of Israel), and Daniel (who was promoted to the third ruler in the kingdom), the prize (God's favor) is well worth the price!

II Corinthians 4:17 says *"for our light affliction, which is but for a moment, worketh for us a far more exceeding and eternal weight of glory; while we look not at the things which are seen, but at the things which are not seen: for the things which are seen are temporal; but the things which are not seen are eternal."* When you find yourself paying the price for having God's favor remember that the circumstances you are facing are temporary and they are producing for you a glory that: (1) cannot be compared to anything else, (2) outweighs the problems you may be facing and (3) will last forever!

Life is often lonely and isolating when paying the price for having God's favor, but there are many biblical principles you can use to fight and defeat the enemy as you face the challenges of having God's favor. Listed below are five of those principles.

Principle 1: Trust

Jeremiah 29:11 says *"for I know the thoughts that I think toward you, saith the Lord, thoughts of peace, and not of evil, to give you an expected end."* It is easy to trust God when we're enjoying the privileges of favor but not as easy when we're paying the price. As we walk through seasons that require us to pay the price for having God's favor, remember that it's only for a season, and even though it may not seem like it, we must trust that God is working all things together for our good, and using our circumstances to prepare us for the "expected end" He has planned for our life. If we can trust God for our salvation, we can trust Him for everything else.

Principle 2: Focus on God's Presence

When we're paying the price for having God's favor, it's easy to focus on our problems instead of God's presence. The enemy knows that if he can shift our attention away from God's presence and cause us to focus on our problems, then he can defeat us by convincing us that we've been forgotten and forsaken by God. But it's important for us to remember that no matter what's going on in our life, the Lord is always with us.

Isaiah 43:2 says *"when thou passest through the waters, **I will be with thee**: and through the rivers, they shall not overflow thee: when thou walkest through the fire, thou shalt not be burned: neither shall the flame kindle upon thee."* When we focus on God's presence, we are reminded that we are never alone. We are reminded that God is always there to strengthen, comfort, and reassure us during challenging seasons.

Principle 3: Guard Your Thoughts

If we let the enemy control our thoughts, he will control our life. Our mind is a constant battleground between good and evil so we must guard our thoughts and keep them aligned with the Word of God. The Bible gives us a principle to help us keep our thoughts aligned with God's Word. *Philippians 4:8* says *"finally, brethren, whatsoever things are true, whatsoever things are honest, whatsoever things are just, whatsoever things are pure, whatsoever things are lovely, whatsoever things are good report; if there be any virture, and if there be any praise, think on these things."*

We should guard our thoughts by meditating daily on God's Word. If we keep our mind saturated with the wise and godly thoughts of Philippians 4:8, we will defeat the enemy in the battleground of our mind and walk in victory in a season he intended for defeat.

Principle 4: Let God Fight For You

When people do us wrong, our natural instinct is to retaliate quickly and fiercely, which is exactly what the enemy wants us to do. But if we're going to overcome the attacks and tactics of the enemy, we must understand that our battles belong to God. *II Chronicles 20:15* reminds us to… *"be not afraid nor dismayed by reason of this great multitude; for the battle is not yours but God's."* I know it can be hard to do, but when you're being talked about, criticized, lied on, rejected, overlooked, etc. because you have God's favor, don't retaliate, let God fight for you. He's undefeated!

Principle 5: Keep Pressing

I Corinthians 15:58 says *"therefore, my beloved brethren, be ye steadfast, unmoveable, always abounding in the work of the Lord, forasmuch as ye know that your labor is not in vain in the Lord."* Have you ever wondered if the price was worth the prize? I have, especially when it seems like I've been paying the price more than enjoying the prize. As I stated earlier, at times, the price of favor can lead to a lonely and isolating walk. But we should be encouraged to know that our labor for God is not in vain. When you know the enemy is attacking you in every way he can, keep pressing and never give up. The price of favor is high, but the price is well worth the prize!

FAVOR: God's Exception to the Rule

Father in the name of Jesus, I declare that You are a God of mercy and You make all things well concerning me. You said in Isaiah 58:11 that You are "the Lord that will guide me always, satisfy my needs in a sun scorched land and strengthen my frame..." Lord, I thank You for overturning the verdict of the enemy for my good. I thank You for overruling decrease, sickness, and demotion, and for making the impossible possible. You said I will be "like a well watered garden, like a spring whose waters never fail. Because Your favor is the exception to the rule, I will walk through this season of favor with joy, peace, and thankfulness of heart. In Jesus name, Amen.

Chapter 4

FAVOR: God's Exception to the Rule

"The king's heart is in the hand of the Lord, as the rivers of water: He turneth it withersoever He will" (Proverbs 21:1).

When favor is on assignment, it has the ability to overrule the laws of man. It is never confined or limited by earthly rules, regulations, policies or procedures. In fact, for the child of God who is on assignment, favor is often the exception to the rule. When man says one thing, favor says another. Men have their say, but favor has the final say!

Now, before we go any further, let's define the word exception. An exception is an instance or situation that does not conform to the general rule. It is an interruption in the normal or usual process. In today's society, the normal or usual process uses our past and our present to determine our future. It uses systems and methods created by man to determine who is and isn't qualified for the promotion, the raise, the scholarship, the

FAVOR: God's Exception to the Rule

loan and a multitude of other things. But when these rules, regulations, policies and procedures begin to interfere with God's plan, He allows favor to come on the scene, work on our behalf and overrule what the systems and methods of man said could not, and would not be done. Why? So His will can be accomplished in the earth.

In other words, favor disrupts the status quo to put us in position to fulfill our purpose. Because favor is God's exception to the rule, it is more powerful than the training, experience, education, credit score, test score, etc. man says we need to progress and move forward in life. Favor causes things to happen that man cannot explain. For example, the policy states that the lowest bid wins the contract, but favor works to get you the contract (even though your bid was the highest) because God knows you'll work with integrity and honesty.

The guidelines say you need a certain GPA along with a certain ACT/SAT score to get the scholarship, but God used favor to cause the scholarship committee to make an exception on your behalf because they see the potential in you to excel in college if given the opportunity to attend. The policy states that the bank can't approve a business loan for the amount you requested because your annual income doesn't meet the requirement, but favor stepped in and touched the load officer's heart to approve your business loan so you can move forward with the vision God gave you.

When favor is operating in our life, it opens doors that others wouldn't, gives us promotions we aren't qualified for, causes our enemies to bless us, and it works supernaturally in other areas of our life as God allows. People may doubt what you say, but they cannot doubt what they see; and when they begin to see how God allows His favor to operate in your life, they will know that God's hand is on your life.

As God's Exception to the Rule, favor is a game changer! It tips the scales in our favor and allows us to experience victory when we should have experienced defeat. When God endorses us with His favor, we cannot be defeated, and we cannot be denied.

FAVOR: God's Exception to the Rule

Father in the name of Jesus, I thank You for the opportunities You are giving me to possess what You have declared belongs to me. Your Word says in Genesis 39:21 "but the Lord was with Joseph, and shewed him mercy, and gave him favor in the sight of the keeper of the prison. Lord, as you did with Joseph, I ask You to show me mercy and give me favor in the sight of those who are a part of Your plan for my life. Grant me access to the right people, at the right time so Your will can be accomplished in my life. In Jesus name, Amen.

Chapter 5

Access Granted: The Influence of Favor

"And it was so, when the king saw Esther the queen standing in the court, that she obtained favor in his sight: and the king held out to Esther the golden scepter that was in his hand. So Esther drew near, and touched the top of the scepter" (Esther 5:2).

From the day we were born until this present moment, we are influenced by the things we see, hear, read, smell, touch, taste and say. Some of those influences were insignificant and temporary, they've come and gone without a second thought; but there were also influences that made such an impression on us that they're still with us today. Influence is a powerful force, it has the power to alter the course of history and impact countless generations; but as powerful as it is, influence does not work along. Influence is leveraged by favor.

FAVOR: God's Exception to the Rule

Walking in the favor of God produces a realm of divine influence that, at the appointed time, brings everything and everyone under the authority of God's divine assignment for our life. The book of Esther gives us a clear picture of the power of influence and the impact it can have. There is no doubt that Esther had favor, but she didn't operate in influence until an appointed time. At God's appointed time, the favor on Esther's life allowed her to operate in a realm of influence that saved a nation.

The favor of God positions us in the right place at the right time, and gives us the ability to walk in influence. Our ability to influence others should never be taken for granted, especially when it comes to the things of God. Influence is not something that should be used as a tool for personal gain or selfish ulterior motives. It should be used to benefit others and to advance God's agenda so His will can be accomplished in the earth.

It was the influence that allowed Esther to petition the king for a decree that would allow the Jews to defend themselves against a plot that was written to take their lives. It was the influence of Naaman's servant that convinced him to follow Elisha's instructions to dip in the Jordan river seven times to be healed of his leprosy. After spying out the land, it was the influence of Joshua and Caleb that assured Moses that the

Access Granted: The Influence of Favor

children of Israel could defeat their enemies and possess the land of Canaan which God promised them. Favor allows us to tap into a real of influence that can turn the heart of a heathen king; humble the attitude of a prideful leader, and embolden two spies to give a report to their leader that would require the children of Israel to walk by faith and not by sight.

Influence may not always look like you think it will look, but it will always accomplish what it has been assigned to accomplish. Influence and favor work hand in hand to help us finish the work God has assigned us to do. We should always remember that God allows us to operate in influence to build His kingdom, and fulfill His purpose for our lives.

FAVOR: God's Exception to the Rule

Lord, I thank You for giving me the opportunity to partake in your principles of favor. As I seek Your wisdom, I ask that you would prosper my mind to pursue, understand, and obey these principles. Father, help me to maintain a consistent commitment to walk in the principles You have given me this day. Father, You said in Proverbs 3:5 "so shalt thou find favor and good understanding in the sight of God and man. Lord, as I purpose in my heart to obey Your principles, I declare that I will walk in a life of favor and victory. In Jesus name, Amen!

Chapter 6

Principles of Favor

"All scripture is given by inspiration of God, and is profitable for doctrine, for reproof, for correction, for instruction in righteousness: that the man of God may be perfect, thoroughly furnished unto all good works" (II Timothy 3:16-17).

The Bible, which is the Christian's guidebook through life, is the final authority for all things. It is the source by which God provides instructions, principles, and guidelines for His children. If we follow God's instructions and correctly apply His principles, we can receive and maintain the blessings and promises God has prepared for our lives. In this chapter, *Principles of Favor*, I will share ten Biblical principles that should be implemented in our daily lives in order to maintain the favor God has given us to be successful in our assignment.

FAVOR: God's Exception to the Rule

Principle 1: Obedience

"…And keep the charge of the Lord thy God, to walk in His ways, to keep His statues, and His commandments, and His judgments, and His testimonies, as it is written in the law of Moses, that thou mayest prosper in all that thou doest…" (I Kings 2:3).

Whenever we disobey God, we are willingly participating in the enemy's plan to destroy us and separate us from God. True obedience means doing what God says, when He says it, how He says it should be done, until what He says is accomplished. The Lord calls us to obedience so we can enjoy the abundant life and receive all that He has in store for us. Obedience ALWAYS brings blessings

Principle 2: Preparation

"Study to show thyself approved unto God, a workman that needeth not to be ashamed, rightly dividing the Word of truth" (II Timothy 2:15)

There is power in preparation! Favor is manifested when preparation meets opportunity. Study God's Word and prepare yourself for God's purpose for your life. Getting prepared is our job, bringing it to pass is God's job. If we prepare for favor (in connection with our purpose), God will bring it to pass.

Principle 3: Position.

"Then the king made Daniel a great man, and gave him many great gifts, and made him ruler over the whole province of Babylon, and chief of the governors over all the wise men of Babylon. **Then Daniel requested of the king, and he set Sha'drach, Me'shach, and Abednego, over the affairs of the province of Babylon:** *but Daniel sat in the gate of the king"* (Daniel 2:48-49).

God will allow His favor to position us in places of authority so His favor can flow through us to be a blessing to others. When *"the king made Daniel a great man,"* Daniel didn't forget about his three friends who were taken into captivity with him. When Daniel was promoted to a higher position, he used the favor that was on his life to secure a higher position for Sha'drach, Me'shac and Abednego. God positions us to be a blessing to others.

Principle 4: Humility

"Humble yourselves therefore under the mighty hand of God, that He may exalt you in due time" (I Peter 5:6).

Humility is not weakness or uncertainty, it is deliberate submission to the will of God. We often spend too much time with an exaggerated sense of self importance. This allows pride to come in and cause us to focus more on ourselves than on Christ. As long as we are prideful, we cannot know God in His fullness. Humble yourself, and God will exalt you at the appointed time.

Principle 5: Trust

"Blessed is the man that trusteth in the Lord, and whose hope the Lord is. For he shall be as a tree planted by the waters, and that spreadeth out her roots by the river, and shall not see when heat cometh, but her leaf shall be green; and shall not be careful in the year of drought, neither shall cease from yielding fruit" (Jeremiah 17:7-8).

Trusting God means looking beyond what we can see to what God sees. Although we don't know what tomorrow will bring, God does; and we must trust that He is working things out on our behalf in ways we cannot see. The challenges we're facing may be great, but our God is greater!

Principle 6: Integrity

Biblical integrity is not just doing the right thing; it's having the right heart while doing the right thing. When you operate in integrity, you are the same person in private that you are in public. Integrity provides a safe path through life and allows God to bless the works of your hands.

Principle 7: Honesty

"Providing for honest things, not only in the sight of the Lord, but also in the sight of men" (II Corinthians 8:21).

When you walk in the principle of honesty, you cannot and will not compromise the Word of God. Honesty is essential if the favor of God is to continue operating in our life. When we say we are Christians, our level of honesty has a strong influence on how others perceive the God we serve, especially non-believers. If we are dishonest in our dealings with man, God cannot trust us to walk in honesty with the favor He has given us.

FAVOR: God's Exception to the Rule

Principle 8: Wisdom

"How much better is it to get wisdom than gold! And to get understanding rather to be chosen than silver" (Proverbs 16:16).

Wisdom gives us the ability to see things from God's perspective and respond according to Biblical principles. Walking in wisdom allows us to receive God's direction for our lives. It saves us from many difficulties, equips us to handle difficult circumstances and positions us to receive eternal rewards.

Principle 9: Stewardship

"Moreover it is required in stewards, that a man be found faithful" (I Corinthians 4:2).

The main idea of stewardship is this: God owns everything, and we are simply managers of ALL (our time, gifts, money, talents, etc) that He has given us. Stewardship is the commitment of ourselves and our possessions to God's service. We must learn how to become responsible stewards of God's resources and manage them to the best of our ability. One day we will give an account to God as to how well we walked in and managed His resources. Let us manage the favor God has given us with EXCELLENCE!

Principle 10: Divine Connections/Relationships

"Be ye not unequally yoked together with unbelievers: for what fellowship hath righteousness with unrighteousness? And what communion hath light with darkness" (II Corinthians 6:14).

When the favor of God is on your life, you must be mindful of the people you associate with. God has already prepared divine connections/relationships for us, to help strengthen and equip us for our assignment. The people God connects us to will be an asset, not a hindrance to the favor He has given us. Guard your favor by connecting to the right people.

Walking in Biblical principles spare us from making many missteps and mistakes. They help us stay on the path God has prepared for our lives and guide us on our journey so we can impact the world for Christ!

FAVOR: God's Exception to the Rule

Father in the name of Jesus, I ask you to touch me right now. Give me sight beyond the norm to recognize the favor You have placed on my life. You said in I Corinthians 2:9 that "eye hath not seen, nor ear heard, neither have entered into the heart of man, the things which God hath prepared for them that love Him." Lord, I ask that You would pour out your Spirit upon me as I seek You every day. In Jesus name, Amen.

Chapter 7

The Finishing Touch

"And in the morning, rising up a great while before day, He (Jesus) went out, and departed into a solitary place, and there prayed" (Mark 1:35).

This chapter, *The Finishing Touch* is designed as a two week devotional. As you prayerfully read each day's devotion, take a moment to listen to what the Holy Spirit says to you as it relates to each confession and scripture. As He speaks, write what He says under Today's Reflection. Pray about what the Spirit has said to you, and ask Him to help you walk in and implement the things He has spoken to your heart.

Day 1 Scripture

"For thou, Lord, will bless the righteous; with favor will thou compass him as with a shield" (Psalm 5:12).

Today's Confession

I declare this day that the Lord will surround me with His shield of favor. God will comfort me on every side.

Today's Reflection

_____

_____

_____

_____

_____

Day 2 Scripture

"Thou shalt arise, and have mercy upon Zion: for the time to favor her, yea, the set time, is come" (Psalm 102:13)

Today's Confession

God's favor is fully operating in my life. Thank you for this time You have chosen to manifest Your mighty works. You said if I so decree a thing it shall be established.

Today's Reflection

_____

_____

_____

_____

_____

Day 3 Scripture

"Blessed shalt thou be when thou comest in, and blessed shalt thou be when thou goest out" (Deuteronomy 28:6).

Today's Confession

God's Favor covers me in all my endeavors. When I come in and when I go out, God will cover me with His favor.

Today's Reflection

_____

_____

_____

_____

_____

Day 4 Scripture

"Surely goodness and mercy shall follow me all the days of my life: and I will dwell in the house of the Lord forever" (Psalm 23:6).

Today's Confession

Because of God's goodness and kindness, I will continually dwell with Him.

Today's Reflection

_____

_____

_____

_____

_____

_____

Day 5 Scripture

"O my God, I trust in thee: let me not be ashamed, let not mine enemies triumph over me" (Psalm 25:2).

Today's Confession

Because of God's favor, my victories come with ease. My enemies stumble and fall before me because of God's protection

Today's Reflection

_____

_____

_____

_____

_____

Day 6 Scripture

"By this I know that thou favourest me, because mine enemy doth not triumph over me" (Psalm 41:11).

Today's Confession

God's favor covers me from my enemies, they will not triumph over me. Lord, you are a God who won't let me be made ashamed.

Today's Reflection

_____
_____
_____
_____
_____

Day 7 Scripture

"For the Lord God is a sun and shield: the Lord will give grace and glory: no good thing will he withhold from them that walk uprightly" (Psalm 84:11)

Today's Confession

No good thing will God withhold from me. Whatever state I'm in, God's favor will be with me.

Today's Reflection

_____

_____

_____

_____

_____

Day 8 Scripture

"For whoso findeth me findeth life, and shall obtain favor of the Lord" (Proverbs 8:35).

Today's Confession

I will seek the Lord daily with my whole heart, and early will I rise to bless His name. I will worship the Lord with my whole heart.

Today's Reflection

_____

_____

_____

_____

_____

Day 9 Scripture

"The Lord shall open unto thee His good treasure, the heaven to give the rain unto thy land in His season, and to bless all the work of thine hand…" (Deuteronomy 28:12a)

Today's Confession

Today, God's favor opens doors no man can shut. Whatsoever door I put my hands to, God will bless and multiply.

Today's Reflection

_____
_____
_____
_____
_____

Day 10 Scripture

"I will say of the Lord, He is my refuge and my fortress: my God; in Him will I trust. Surely He shall deliver thee from the snare of the fowler, and from the noisome pestilence" (Psalm 91:2-3).

Today's Confession

God's grace and mercy is forever with me. For the Lord will rescue me from any snare.

Today's Reflection

_____
_____
_____
_____
_____

Day 11 Scripture

"And all these blessings shall come on thee, and overtake thee, if thou shalt hearken unto the voice of the Lord thy God" (Deuteronomy 28:2).

Today's Confession

Because of my obedience, favor will be released to me this day.

Today's Reflection

_____
_____
_____
_____
_____

The Finishing Touch

Day 12 Scripture

"And let the beauty of the Lord our God be upon us: and establish thou the work of our hands upon us; yea, the work of our hands establish thou it" (Psalm 90:17).

Today's Confession

I will prosper in my works because God has favored the works of my hands.

Today's Reflection

_____

_____

_____

_____

_____

Day 13 Scripture

"The Lord bless thee, and keep thee; the Lord make His face shine upon thee, and be gracious unto thee: The Lord lift up His countenance upon thee, and give thee peace. And they shall put my name upon the children of Israel; and I will bless them" (Numbers 6:24-27).

Today's Confession

God's favor is blessing me with what I did not seek. He shall make His face shine upon me and be gracious to me.

Today's Reflection

_____

_____

_____

_____

_____

Day 14 Scripture

"Blessed be the Lord, who daily loadeth us with benefits, even the God of our salvation. Se'lah." (Psalm 68:19).

Today's Confession

God makes His face to shine upon me daily. Favor is daily loaded to every area of my life.

Today's Reflection

_____

_____

_____

_____

_____

Closing Prayer

Father in the name of Jesus, I thank You that by Your favor You have made me strong. I thank You for the wisdom, knowledge, and understanding of favor you have given me. I thank You that my eyes have been enlightened on the importance of what it takes to obtain, and maintain a favor filled life in and from You. Lord, I thank you that if I live to please You, and obey Your Word, Your favor on my life will last a lifetime. In Jesus name, Amen!

About the Author

Minister Rolanda Gibson has an unwavering commitment to the Lord Jesus Christ, the integrity of His Holy Word, and a love for His people! Minister Gibson, a native of Baton Rouge, Louisiana is founder and CEO of Rolanda Gibson Ministries and DIAMONDS Leadership Academy (DLA) which is a non-profit organization for young ladies in grades 6th-12th.

Answering her call to ministry at the age of 17, Minister Gibson has over 20 years of ministry experience. Her ministry experience includes service as an Associate Pastor, Youth Pastor, Adult Bible Study and Sunday School Teacher. Minister Gibson has been privileged to minister at numerous youth and adult workshops and conferences.

Minister Gibson boldly declares the Word of God with uncompromised accuracy, clarity, power and authority. She is an anointed teacher and preacher who rightly divides the Word of God and is adamant about using God's Word to educate, equip, empower and impact the lives of others to live their best life now.

FAVOR: God's Exception to the Rule

Her desire and call to teach and preach has provided her with many opportunities to share the Gospel of Jesus Christ with people of all ages. Minister Gibson believes *"the Spirit of the Lord is upon her, because He has anointed her to preach the Gospel to the poor; He has sent her to heal the broken-hearted, to preach deliverance to the captives, and recovering of sight to the blind, to set at liberty them that are bruised, to preach the acceptable year of the Lord"* (Luke 4:18-19).

Additional Books by Minister Gibson

Now I Know

The King's Daughter

To Contact the Author

Visit our website: RolandaGibsonMinistries.com. Write Rolanda Gibson Ministries at P.O. Box 74724, Baton Rouge, LA 70874; email: rgibsonministries@gmail.com or call (225) 372-8571

About the Author

Minister Shenetha Caldwell is a Minister of the Gospel, Worship Leader, and Mother. She is called to motivate, revelate, empower, uplift, and help change the lives of others by exemplifying Godly character and re-directing sinners back to Christ. Minister Caldwell believes the greatest thing she has done was to give God a 'yes!'

www.ingramcontent.com/pod-product-compliance
Lightning Source LLC
Chambersburg PA
CBHW051708090426
42736CB00013B/2598